TPM for
Every Operator

SHOPFLOOR SERIES

TPM for
Every Operator

Edited by the Japan Institute of Plant Maintenance

Productivity Press
Portland, Oregon

Originally published as *Yoku wakaru TPM shiriizu: watashitachi no TPM,* © 1988, 1992 by Japan Institute of Plant Maintenance.

English translation © 1996 by Productivity Press, a division of Productivity, Inc. Translated by Andrew P. Dillon.

Productivity Press
P.O. Box 13390
Portland, OR 97213-0390
United States of America
Telephone: 503-235-0600
Telefax: 503-235-0909
E-mail: service@ppress.com

Cover design by William Stanton
Cover illustration by Gary Ragaglia
Graphic revisions, page design, and composition by Rohani Design, Edmonds, Washington
Printed and bound by BookCrafters in the United States of America

Library of Congress Cataloging-in-Publication Data

Yoku wakaru TPM shiriizu. English.
    TPM for every operator / edited by the Japan Institute of Plant
    Maintenance ; publisher's message by Norman Bodek.
        p. cm. -- (Shopfloor series)
    Includes bibliographical references (p.).
    ISBN 1-56327-080-3
    1. Total productive maintenance. I. Nihon Puranto Mentenansu Kyōkai.
    II. Title. III. Series.
TS192. Y65   1996
658.2'02—dc20   96-3138
                                                              CIP

02 01 00 99 98 97 96 10 9 8 7 6 5 4 3 2

Contents

CHAPTER 4: AUTONOMOUS MAINTENANCE 61

CHAPTER 5: TEAM ACTIVITIES 81

CHAPTER 6: TPM AND SAFETY 101

Publisher's Message

Total productive maintenance (TPM) is a world class manufacturing initiative for optimizing the effectiveness of manufacturing equipment. One of the basic principles of TPM is that operators are the first line of defense against unplanned equipment downtime. Operators and others in daily contact with equipment can use their knowledge and familiarity with operating conditions to predict and prevent breakdowns and other equipment-related losses. They do this through regular cleaning and inspection of equipment, and through team-based autonomous maintenance activities that tackle equipment-related problems.

TPM for Every Operator teaches operators and team leaders the key concepts of TPM to support companywide participation—the hallmark of the TPM approach. Six illustrated chapters tell what TPM is and how it benefits operators in particular. An outline overview introduces each chapter, and chapter summaries review key points for discussion and application sessions.

Chapter 1 defines TPM and its five major components. Operators play a particularly important role in the preventive maintenance aspect of TPM—avoiding equipment breakdowns. This chapter introduces the goals and key strategies of TPM, and explains why you need TPM the most when you are the busiest.

Chapter 2 offers advice on using machines efficiently. The result of TPM should be to increase overall equipment effectiveness (OEE). OEE goes up when you eliminate the "six big losses": breakdowns, setup loss, minor stoppages, reduced speed, defects and rework, and startup and yield loss. Operators can help eliminate these six losses simply by questioning small everyday annoyances before they become big problems. Asking "why" several times uncovers the root causes of problems.

Chapter 3 talks about breakdowns, many of which are preventable. Accelerated deterioration shortens equipment life, but often it can be avoided through preventive maintenance activities performed by operators familiar with the machines. The components of preventive maintenance are introduced, with pointers on how *not* to break equipment.

Chapter 4 describes autonomous maintenance, the operator-based approach that is the foundation of TPM. Autonomous maintenance is implemented in seven steps, beginning with cleaning and inspection, followed by elimination of problems and maintenance obstacles. Standards are drawn up for cleaning and lubrication. Next is general inspection, in which operators, engineers, and technicians learn together what is required for optimum efficiency, then develop a checklist to keep equipment in that condition. In the final stages, operators conduct their own checklist inspections and standardize improvements. This chapter also describes tagging—placing tags on equipment problem spots to make them visible, then systematically removing the tags after the root cause of the problem is eliminated.

Chapter 5 teaches basic points of TPM team activities: selecting leaders, setting team goals, learning from management audits, and publicizing results. It introduces three secret weapons for battling loss: activity boards, team meetings, and one-point lessons.

Chapter 6 shows how TPM improves safety on the job. Basic TPM activities such as cleaning and inspection make it harder for difficulty, dirt, and danger to find their way into the workplace. Autonomous maintenance activities systematically eliminate the minor problems and unsafe conditions that turn into breakdowns and accidents. Awareness training and coordinated teamwork help employees recognize and avoid unsafe behaviors.

The text is followed by a brief list of books for further reading on TPM and related subjects.

TPM for Every Operator is part of the Productivity Press Shopfloor Series, a set of short books that condense key information on important manufacturing topics for operators, team leaders, and supervisors. This book is a companion volume to *TPM Team Guide,* which presents the basic principles of team-based TPM activities for this important audience.

We express our appreciation to JIPM, the original author and publisher, for permitting us to publish this edition of *TPM for Every Operator.* Thanks also to the following who participated in producing the book: Steven Ott, president of Productivity Press; Diane Asay, editor in chief; Andrew P. Dillon, translation; Karen Jones, editorial management; Susan Swanson, production management; Julie Zinkus, proofreading; Bill Stanton, cover design; Gary Ragaglia, cover illustration; and Rohani Design, graphics revisions, page design, and composition.

Norman Bodek
Chairman, Productivity, Inc.

Preface

Total productive maintenance (TPM) is now being applied in every industry in companies around the world. To support TPM implementation, the Japan Institute for Plant Maintenance has developed a wide range of reference books targeting specific levels and functions within companies. This book, which has become particularly popular, is part of a series of books for operators that have won wide acclaim from readers.*

For this edition, JIPM consultants have completely reviewed and revised the book to respond to new developments in TPM. The core of the work still addresses TPM activities in production.

Chapter 1 offers an easy-to-understand overview of TPM. In Chapter 2 we present a straightforward discussion of how to raise

---

* As part of the Shopfloor Series, Productivity Press will publish other books from the JIPM series, addressing autonomous maintenance and focused improvement. See also Kunio Shirose, ed., *TPM Team Guide* (Portland, Ore.: Productivity Press, 1995), also developed by JIPM for shopfloor employees.—Ed.

overall equipment effectiveness (OEE)—the primary goal of TPM. Chapter 3 presents the theory and practice of preventing equipment breakdowns. Chapter 4 explains autonomous maintenance—the shopfloor activities that are the most characteristic feature of TPM. We draw on case studies to illustrate TPM team activities in Chapter 5 and safety issues in Chapter 6.

We hope you will put this book to practical use in your company.

Seiichi Nakajima
Japan Institute of Plant Maintenance

Contributors

Akira Ichikawa
TPM Operations Consultant, Japan Institute of Plant Maintenance

Kazumi Takagi
TPM Operations Consultant, Japan Institute of Plant Maintenance

Yuzo Takebe
TPM Operations Consultant, Japan Institute of Plant Maintenance

Kazuhisa Yamazaki
TPM Operations Consultant, Japan Institute of Plant Maintenance

Takao Izumi
TPM Operations Consultant, Japan Institute of Plant Maintenance

Shinichi Shinozuka
TPM Operations Consultant, Japan Institute of Plant Maintenance

Our TPM

CHAPTER 1

CHAPTER OVERVIEW

Our TPM

- From PM to TPM

- Productive Maintenance

- Preventive Maintenance

- Corrective Maintenance

- Maintenance Prevention

- Breakdown Maintenance

- What Kind of Workplace Suffers from Defects and Equipment Breakdowns?

- Preventive Maintenance Is Health Management for Machines

- A Definition of TPM

- Why Do TPM?

- What Makes TPM Different?

- The Goals of TPM

- The Eight Key Strategies of TPM Development

- Six Big Losses That Lower Equipment Efficiency

- The Busier You Are, the More You Need TPM

- Summary

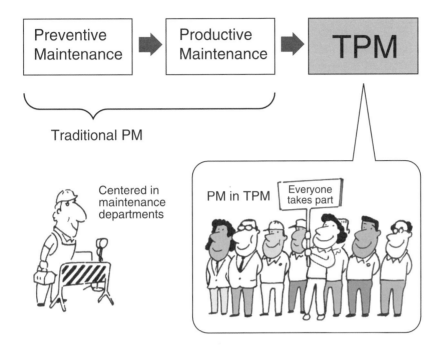

From PM to TPM

Modern equipment management began with *preventive maintenance* and evolved into *productive maintenance.* These approaches—both abbreviated as "PM"—originated in the United States with activities focused in maintenance departments. The two approaches are defined on the next few pages.

TPM stands for *total productive maintenance,* or productive maintenance with total participation. First developed in Japan, TPM is team-based productive maintenance and involves every level and every function in the organization, from top executives to the shop floor.

3

Productive Maintenance

4

Maintaining the equipment that supports production is an important component of any approach to plant maintenance. The goal of productive maintenance is "profitable PM." This requires us not only to prevent breakdowns and defects, but to do so in ways that are efficient and economical. To achieve this goal we need to master four techniques:

- Preventive maintenance—preventing breakdowns

- Corrective maintenance—improving or modifying equipment to prevent breakdowns or to make maintenance easier

- Maintenance prevention—designing and installing equipment that needs little or no maintenance

- Breakdown maintenance—repairing after breakdowns occur

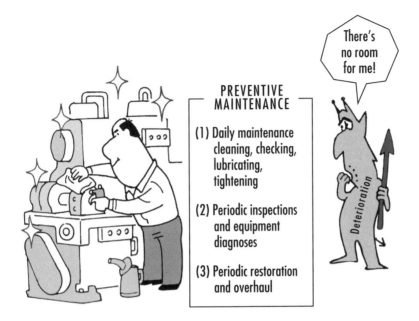

Preventive Maintenance

Sustaining smooth production means avoiding equipment break-downs and defects. We need to install suitable equipment in the first place and to keep it functioning properly. This, in turn, requires three types of activities:

1. Daily maintenance (cleaning, checking, lubricating, and tightening) to prevent deterioration

2. Periodic inspections or equipment diagnoses to measure deterioration

3. Restoration to correct and recover from deterioration

Preventive maintenance means carrying out these three activities.

5

People who use the machine

Breakdown log

Improvement proposals

Improve the design so it doesn't break down

Improve the machine so it's easy to maintain

People who design and maintain the machine

Corrective Maintenance

Corrective maintenance is the name given to improvements that

- keep equipment from breaking down

- facilitate inspection, repair, and use

- ensure safety

Corrective maintenance requires the people who use equipment to do two things:

- Record the results of daily inspections and the details of all breakdowns

- Actively submit improvement ideas aimed at preventing breakdowns and the conditions that cause them

Based on these breakdown records and improvement ideas, maintenance specialists and equipment designers study recurring problems and improve or modify machines to make them less likely to break down, easy to maintain, and safe.

It's 99.9999....% reliable.
Now THAT's maintenance prevention!

Maintenance Prevention

Maintenance prevention incorporates the ideas developed in the course of productive maintenance in the design of new equipment. It means designing or specifying equipment that doesn't break down and is easy to maintain: equipment that is reliable and maintainable.

Maintenance prevention requires us to study maintenance data and to develop "maintenance-free" designs for equipment that doesn't break down (or, if it does, can be repaired easily) and that is easy to use, safe, and inexpensive.

To achieve this, operators and maintenance people need to record maintenance-related information about equipment currently in use in a form that will be helpful to the people who design equipment.

8

Breakdown Maintenance

Breakdown maintenance is the repair of equipment after a breakdown or deterioration in performance.

There are two kinds of breakdown maintenance:

- *Planned repairs* are carried out when it is more economical to deal with a problem after the machine has failed than to prevent the failure.

- *Unplanned repair* involves failures would have been better to prevent. This kind of repair puts the production schedule at risk and is often carried out in panic.

What Kind of Workplace Suffers from Defects and Equipment Breakdowns?

Workplaces plagued by numerous defects and breakdowns have several features in common:

9

- The equipment is filthy and stays that way.

- Oil and lubricant leaks are common and lubricators are empty.

- Rotating parts and moving surfaces are encrusted with chips and raw materials.

- Wires and hoses are tangled and you can't tell what is connected where.

- Equipment mechanisms are hidden by big covers and you can't see inside.

- Materials, parts, tools, and supplies are strewn randomly and you can't tell what is essential and what is not.

- Everyone is utterly convinced that things have to be that way.

Preventive Maintenance Is Health Management for Machines

To keep our bodies in shape, we exercise, watch what we eat and drink, and visit the doctor for periodic health checkups. If we get sick, we treat the problem as soon as possible. All this seems like common sense to us.

Preventive maintenance is really health management for machines. Equipment will stay healthy and run without problems when we give it

- daily maintenance to prevent deterioration

- inspections to measure deterioration

- regular operating checkups

- early treatment to correct the effects of deterioration

What is TPM?

1. The goal of TPM is to build a robust enterprise by maximizing production system efficiency (overall effectiveness).

2. TPM addresses the entire production system life cycle and builds a concrete, shopfloor-based system to prevent all losses. Its aims include the elimination of all accidents, defects, and breakdowns.

3. TPM involves all departments, from production to development, sales, and administration.

4. Everyone participates in TPM, from top executives to shopfloor employees.

5. TPM achieves zero losses through overlapping team activities.

A Definition of TPM

11

The standard definition of TPM is given in the box above. But how does this apply to the production shop floor? Basically, it means

1. Setting the goal of *maximizing equipment effectiveness*

2. Establishing a total PM system focusing on the *entire equipment life cycle*

3. *Coordinating all departments,* including those that design, maintain, and use equipment

4. *Involving everyone,* from top executives to shopfloor employees

5. Managing through *team-based activities* aimed at plantwide goals of *zero losses.*

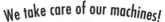

Why Do TPM?

As equipment becomes more automated and sophisticated, it is no exaggeration to say that machines make the product. The role of people, then, is to maintain machines so that they work properly—with no breakdowns and no defects.

But this can't happen when only maintenance specialists are involved as in the past. Total productive maintenance requires the participation of equipment users and equipment and product designers. It is especially important for users (operators) to take an active role in caring for their own equipment to prevent breakdowns and defects.

What Makes TPM Different?

TPM takes the idea of productive maintenance or profitable PM one step further. It moves beyond traditional maintenance activities and involves all departments and employees in equipment management.

Perhaps the most distinctive aspect of TPM is *autonomous maintenance*. Carried out by production floor employees, autonomous maintenance activities help the people take care of their own machines.

Another feature of TPM is that it aims at the *total elimination* of all losses, or zero losses. The insistence on *total* elimination is a key factor in maximizing overall equipment effectiveness (OEE). This concept is crucial in developing a TPM program, and is explained further in Chapter 2.

The Goals of TPM

TPM aims to build healthier companies by strengthening people as well as equipment.

Our workplaces are riddled with equipment-related losses. But what we see on the shop floor is the natural result of the attitudes and behavior of the people who work there—from top managers to frontline workers. The assumptions of the past—that the current state of affairs must be accepted or that breakdowns and defects are outside our control—will never allow us to get rid of all losses.

It follows that to enhance our equipment and to eliminate breakdowns, defects, and other losses, we need to strengthen the skills of every employee. Developing stronger employees and equipment builds a stronger, more resilient company.

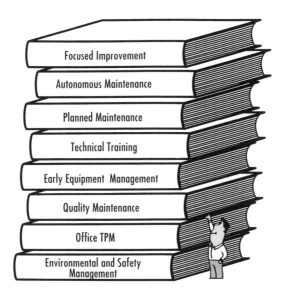

The 8 Key Strategies of TPM Development

Achieving the goals of TPM requires activities in eight key areas:

1. Focused improvement (kaizen) to make equipment more efficient

2. Autonomous maintenance activities

3. Planned maintenance for the maintenance department

4. Technical training in equipment maintenance and oper-ation

5. An early equipment management program

6. Quality maintenance activities

7. A system for increasing the efficiency of administrative and support functions (office TPM)

8. A system for management of safety and environmental issues

Not all of these strategies are implemented at once; each company will develop a sequence that fits its situation. This book concentrates on those activities carried out by equipment operators: autonomous maintenance, focused improvement, and safety activities.

Six Big Losses That Lower Equipment Efficiency

People use machines to produce goods. When equipment doesn't work the way we want, productivity slumps and we end up struggling with overtime or weekend work.

Equipment problems drain productivity in six ways, called the *six big losses*:

1. Breakdowns

2. Setup and adjustment loss

3. Idling and minor stoppages

4. Reduced speed

5. Defects and rework

6. Startup and yield loss

A TPM development program consists of activities aimed specifically at eradicating these six big losses.

16

The Busier You Are, the More You Need TPM

Some readers may be thinking, "We're too busy for TPM." But many busy production workers wish they could make the product more easily and with fewer problems.

High production demand isn't the only reason we feel short of time. Other things intensify the feeling of pressure. Common reasons include equipment idled by breakdowns, the need to rework or reprocess defective parts, and the inability to maintain quality when speed is increased.

Consider this: only when we feel we don't have enough time will improving efficiency make a difference. If we had all the time in the world, we wouldn't need to improve.

The conclusion is clear: TPM is most valuable when we are busiest.

17

CHAPTER SUMMARY

Maintaining the equipment that supports production is an important component of any approach to plant maintenance. TPM is an important approach for keeping production equipment running smoothly and efficiently, without abnormalities or product defects.

TPM stands for *total productive maintenance*—productive maintenance with total participation. TPM is team-based and involves every level and every function in the organization. Equipment operators—the people who use the machines every day— play an especially important role in TPM.

The standard definition of TPM has five main principles:

1. Setting the goal of *maximizing equipment effectiveness* to improve productivity

2. Establishing a total PM system focusing on the *entire equipment life cycle*

3. *Coordinating all departments,* including those that design, maintain, and use equipment

4. *Involving everyone,* from top executives to shopfloor employees

5. Managing through *team-based activities* aimed at plantwide goals of *zero losses.*

The goal of TPM is zero breakdowns and zero losses. It achieves this through *preventive maintenance* (preventing breakdowns), *corrective maintenance* (modifying equipment to prevent breakdowns or make maintenance easier), *maintenance prevention* (designing and installing equipment that needs little maintenance), and *breakdown maintenance* (repairs).

Preventive maintenance is like health management for machines. It involves

- daily maintenance to prevent deterioration

- inspections to measure deterioration

- regular operating checkups

- early treatment to correct the effects of deterioration

Equipment operators are the key to effective preventive maintenance.

A TPM program includes activities to get rid of *six big losses* that drain productivity. These losses are described thoroughly in Chapter 2.

TPM is most valuable when we are busiest. Some employees may think that they are "too busy" to do TPM. When we consider the hassles of dealing with broken equipment, rework, or machines slowed by abnormalities, we realize that high production demand isn't the only source of stress. It is only when we feel we don't have enough time that improving equipment efficiency will make a difference.

19

Using Machines Efficiently

CHAPTER 2

CHAPTER OVERVIEW

Using Machines Efficiently

- What Are the Six Big Losses?
- You Can't Make Products When the Equipment Breaks Down
- Setups and Adjustments Take Too Long
- The Smallest Thing Can Shut Down a Machine
- Running Equipment Faster Causes Defects
- Are You Making Defective Products?
- It Takes Time to Get Started in the Morning
- OEE: An Indicator of Equipment Health
- Which Loss Is the Worst Offender?
- "This Isn't Too Bad"—A Phrase That Invites Losses
- Eradicating Minor Defects Yields Big Profits
- Improvement Begins with Restoration
- Grit and Dust Shorten Equipment Life
- Losses Vanish in Workplaces Where People Ask "Why?"
- Take Care of Your Own Equipment
- Summary

Breakdowns	Setups and adjustments	Idling and minor stoppages

Reduced speed	Defects and rework	Startup and yield loss

What Are the Six Big Losses?

One of the goals of TPM is to use equipment in the most effi-cient way possible. The efficient use of machines makes work easier and our companies more profitable. Using equipment as efficiently as possible means maximizing its functions and perfor-mance. We can increase efficiency by rooting out losses that sap efficiency.

The "six big losses" lower efficiency of production equipment:

1. Breakdowns

2. Setup and adjustment loss

3. Idling and minor stoppages

4. Reduced speed

5. Defects and rework

6. Startup and yield loss

You Can't Make Products When the Equipment Breaks Down

You have a full production schedule and your equipment breaks down. The maintenance people are busy and take a long time to show up. So you end up having to work overtime or on weekends.

These are *breakdown losses*. How many hours per month do you lose to this kind of situation at your plant? Perhaps you think it's normal for equipment to break down and that when it does, you—or rather the maintenance department—simply need to fix it. But how often do machines break down because we don't use or care for them correctly?

Setups and Adjustments Take Too Long

Low volume, high diversity production is the norm today. Many companies switch models several times a month—or even several times a day. Lugging around heavy tools and dies wears people out, and tightening and loosening bolts and screws takes time. What's more, delicate adjustments of dimensions and machining conditions call for experience, "feel," and courage: an experienced operator can do the job quickly, but new people take a long time to get it right.

Setup loss refers to the time it takes to change tools and dies. *Adjustment loss* is the additional time it takes to turn out the next good part. As the number of products increases, companies find their setup and adjustment taking more time than actual production. High diversity production is inefficient unless steps are taken to eliminate this loss.

26

The Smallest Thing Can Shut Down a Machine

Sometimes it may seem like an easy job to operate an automatic machine, but what about all those times when parts get stuck in the chute? It may be just a minor problem that doesn't require a maintenance call, but it's still an annoyance that breaks the production flow.

Losses like this are called minor stoppages. People tend to ignore minor stoppages because machine function is easy to restore. But closer examination shows that such stoppages often add up to surprisingly substantial losses. Frequent minor stoppages keep operators busy and frustrated. They also increase the risk of accidents. Eliminating minor stoppages will make work much easier.

Running Equipment Faster Causes Defects

Here's a common story: "The manufacturer's specs say we can run the machine faster and that's what the boss told us to do. But when we tried it, it didn't work—we couldn't hold the tolerances, probably because the machine is old."

We call this loss *reduced speed* or speed loss, and it isn't as inevitable as you might think.

Other types of speed losses involve situations like the following:

- A V-belt slackens and speed drops before anyone notices

- No one knows the design (specification) speed

- No one has ever wondered how fast the machine can run

Sometimes a small improvement can raise equipment speed.

28

Are You Making Defective Products?

"Yesterday we had a run of bad luck. We worked overtime, but inspection showed that we had made a pile of defective parts. When they checked our equipment, they found that precision was off because of a loose clamping bolt on the tool. I guess we can use the parts if we rework them."

These are *defect and rework losses*. Working hard is no excuse for making defective parts. Even if we have only 1 percent defects, a loss is still a loss—it's still a form of waste. And the time we spend reworking parts is waste, too.

It Takes Time to Get Started in the Morning

"In cold weather, it takes quite a while to get machines started up and stabilized. Our hydraulic units run slowly until the oil heats up."

Such losses, called *startup and yield losses,* come about for the same reasons as adjustment losses during setups.

In machining plants, we also need to watch for *tool losses*—the time it takes to change worn tools and the defects and rework time caused by tool breakage.

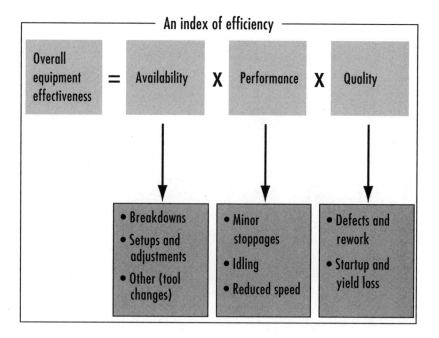

OEE: An Indicator of Equipment Health

TPM uses an index called overall equipment effectiveness (OEE) to clarify the impact of the six big losses and to measure the overall health of equipment.

Here is the formula for determining your OEE:

Overall equipment effectiveness = availability × performance × quality

Taking the six big losses into account and calculating OEE typically yields a figure of 50 percent to 60 percent. In other words, most plants are only using machines to half of their potential.

Improvement Goals for the Six Big Losses

Type of loss	Goal	Explanation
1. Breakdowns	0	Should be zero for all equipment
2. Setups and adjustments	minimize	As short as possible: less than 10 minutes with zero adjustments
3. Reduced speed	0	Should match or—with improvements—exceed equipment specifications
4. Minor stoppages	0	Should be zero for all equipment
5. Defects and rework	0	Extent may vary, but goal should be expressed in parts per million (e.g., between 100 and 30 ppm).
6. Startup loss	minimize	

Which Loss Is the Worst Offender?

Which losses make us busy and make our work harder? To find out, we calculate overall equipment effectiveness and actually find out how much time we are spending on the six big losses. Identify the worst offender (the most damaging of the six big losses) and put a "wanted" poster on your activities board. Arresting these time thieves improves efficiency and gives you time to work.

The chart above tells how far you should pursue elimination of the six big losses.

"This Isn't Too Bad"—A Phrase That Invites Losses

We've identified the most damaging losses. What causes them? Let's consider the case of machine breakdowns.

A part may burn because of insufficient lubricant. No one notices that a belt is about to break. A worn hydraulic hose is overlooked. Minor stoppages and defects keep occurring because of too much play in parts. These are all things that cause losses.

Many problems like this are ignored or overlooked because we think they're "not too bad." We call problems like this *minor defects*. It turns out, though, that minor defects often cause major losses.

Eradicating Minor Defects Yields Big Profits

Minor defects pile up and grow into breakdowns, fatal quality defects, and other big losses. To eradicate the worst offenders (that is, the six major losses), we have to get rid of all the small fry, the minor defects. For this, we need to take the following steps:

1. Find minor defects and other small problems hidden in the equipment and "arrest" them by tagging them.

2. Correct the problems and remove the tags. Have maintenance help with problems we can't fix ourselves.

These activities are explained in detail in Chapter 4, but the bottom line is that correcting seemingly trivial problems eventually leads to big profits.

Changing part dimensions or material won't improve things if hidden defects are the cause.

First restore equipment to its original condition; THEN think about improvements.

Improvement Begins with Restoration

We sometimes alter the dimensions of equipment parts or change raw materials to reduce losses, but nothing improves no matter what we do. Often the problem lies in worn parts, insufficient precision, or play in attachments rather than in the dimensions or materials.

As equipment is used, wear and corrosion cause processing conditions to deteriorate. This is why it is important to *restore* equipment—to return it to its original (ideal) state. When you have lost your way, it is generally surer—and ultimately quicker—to return to your original location rather than to forge blindly ahead.

To get rid of losses, first restore the equipment. Start thinking about equipment or material modifications only if restoration doesn't solve the problem.

Failure to add oil

Water or oil on sensor

Grit and dirt in revolving or sliding parts

Dirt and dust on cooling fan

Grit and Dust Shorten Equipment Life

Equipment deteriorates as you use it, and misuse often hastens deterioration. We call this *accelerated deterioration*. Examples of accelerated deterioration situations include:

- problems due to failure to lubricate where necessary

- failures caused by water or oil in sensors

- excess wear from dirt or grime on rotating or sliding parts

- motor overheating due to dust-clogged cooling fans

In each example, accelerated deterioration shortens the life of parts. This is different from the daily wear and tear that takes place even when equipment is used properly. We call daily wear and tear *natural deterioration*. Once we have gone to the trouble of restoring equipment to its original state, we need to eliminate the causes of accelerated deterioration.

35

Losses Vanish in Workplaces Where People Ask "Why?"

The quickest way to start correcting the problems that cause losses is to understand thoroughly how equipment works and to look at each problem logically. Looking at a problem logically simply means asking "why" at least three times. Let's take an example: defects from an external diameter machining process.

Why? Round 1

The first "why?" takes us from the defect—which is a result—to a clarification of what is actually happening: variability in the finish grind dimensions on the cylindrical grinder.

Why? Round 2

The next "why?" leads us to the equipment's mechanism: the variability in finishing dimensions arises because of variability in the contact point between the grindstone and the material.

Why? Round 3

With the third "why?" we move from the equipment mechanism to questioning the cause of the variability. Is the cause in the machine? The fixture? Defects in the previous process? Or is the machining process at fault?

P-M analysis, an improvement methodology often used in TPM, starts with these steps. (See the Further Reading section for more on P-M analysis.) Asking "why?" is the foundation of all equipment improvement.

Take Care of Your Own Equipment

TPM requires a shift in attitudes toward equipment from the traditional "I make it; you fix it" to "we take care of our own machines." To eliminate the six big losses, participation of equipment operators is essential.

Breakdowns and minor stoppages, in particular, impact the activities of operators—the people who have the most contact with equipment and know it best. In TPM we don't see eliminating breakdowns as a maintenance department responsibility or getting rid of defects as management's job. Everyone participates in reducing losses to zero—and everyone benefits. With total participation, TPM can make the "zero loss" workplace a reality.

CHAPTER SUMMARY

One goal of TPM is to use equipment as efficiently possible, which makes work easier and our companies more profitable. Using equipment efficiently means maximizing its functions and performance. We do this by rooting out six big losses that sap efficiency:

1. Breakdowns

2. Setup and adjustment loss

3. Idling and minor stoppages

4. Reduced speed

5. Defects and rework

6. Startup and yield loss

Equipment *breakdowns* can lose hours of production time. Many breakdowns happen because people don't use or take care of their machines correctly. These kinds of breakdowns are largely avoidable.

Inefficient approaches to changeover lead to *setup and adjustment losses*—equipment downtime, physical exertion, time spent adjusting the new setup, and defects produced before the setup is ready for production. Companies need to fix these losses to produce the diverse products customers require.

Minor stoppages are usually problems that keep automated machines from running unsupervised. Although they may seem like petty annoyances, these short stops keep operators busy and frustrated and increase the chance of an accident.

39

Reduced speed refers to situations where minor abnormalities like loose V-belts keep equipment from running at the speed it was designed for. Repairs and improvements can raise equipment speed.

Product *defects and rework* are unproductive because they waste materials, energy, and our production time.

Startup and yield losses are inefficiencies in getting the machine to produce the first good products—a waste of time, materials, and energy.

Overall equipment effectiveness (OEE) is a formula used in TPM for measuring the impact of the six big losses.

Losses get a foot in the door when people think minor problems "aren't too bad." This attitude allows small problems to turn into major breakdowns, defects, or accidents. The chance of this is increased when we neglect to clean and lubricate our machines, which leads to *accelerated deterioration.*

As you do daily maintenance activities, tag minor problems and annoyances to make them visible. Remove the tags by asking "why" to learn what causes the problem and then taking steps to restore the equipment to its ideal state.

Eliminating Breakdowns

CHAPTER 3

CHAPTER OVERVIEW

Eliminating Breakdowns

- Breakdowns Come in Two Types

- People Cause Breakdowns

- Why Do Machines Fail?

- When Do Breakdowns Happen?

- Two Types of Deterioration

- The Buck Stops Here

- Watch for Slight Abnormalities

- Coming to Grips with Zero Breakdowns

- Providing the Basics (Cleaning and Inspecting, Lubricating, and Tightening)

- Daily Checks Are the First Step of TPM

- Find the Root Cause and Restore the Equipment

- Nip Breakdowns in the Bud with Autonomous Maintenance

- Why General Inspection?

- Learning How Not to Break Equipment

- Learning from Breakdowns

- Summary

Function-loss breakdowns　　　**Function-reduction breakdowns**

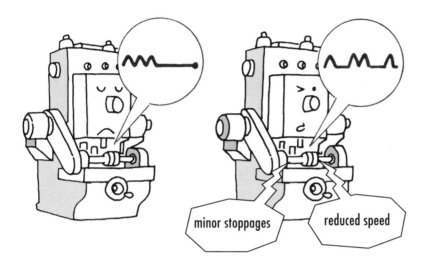

Breakdowns Come in Two Types

Two types of breakdown can occur when a piece of equipment loses a given function or functions:

1. *Function-loss breakdown:* the complete loss of equipment function. This type is also known as a "sporadic" breakdown.

2. *Function-reduction breakdown:* This sort of breakdown occurs when a piece of equipment suffers from some partial loss of function. An example would be a fluorescent light bulb that has grown dimmer and starts to flicker. The machine still runs but experiences losses such as defects, minor stoppages, and reduced speed.

People Cause Breakdowns

44

In most cases, equipment doesn't fail by itself. People often cause breakdowns indirectly by neglecting to do what they should: forgetting to grease bearings or tighten bolts, for example.

Breakdowns are also the result of misguided attitudes—for example, the belief that breakdowns are unavoidable, or that machines are someone else's responsibility, or that maintenance isn't doing its job.

The lesson is clear: equipment doesn't break down by itself; people break it.

Why Do Machines Fail?

Production equipment is composed of vast numbers of bolts, chains, belts, bearings, gears, shafts, cylinders, motors, limit switches, proximity switches and other parts. A piece of equipment runs normally as long as each component performs its assigned function.

Misoperation of equipment and poor maintenance cause stress in individual parts, however, and sooner or later the function of those parts deteriorates. When this happens, the equipment may stop working or it may turn out defective parts. This is how breakdowns are caused.

When Do Breakdowns Happen?

As the chart above shows, breakdowns fall into three distinct categories depending on when they occur during the life of the equipment. These three periods are:

1. Initial breakdown period (after installation breakdowns gradually decrease)

2. Accidental breakdown period (breakdowns remain fairly constant)

3. Wear-related breakdown period (breakdowns gradually increase)

Breakdowns occur in the period of initial equipment use because of errors in design, fabrication, or installation. Those that show up in the accidental breakdown period occur for largely unforeseeable reasons. Wear-related breakdowns are linked to wear and tear and deterioration as the machine ages. Some of this deterioration is natural, but in many cases deterioration is accelerated by our neglect.

Natural deterioration

The fan belt is worn

Accelerated deterioration

Not enough oil!

Two Types of Deterioration

47

Natural deterioration refers to performance losses caused by physical deterioration that occurs over time even when equipment is used correctly.

In *accelerated deterioration,* on the other hand, people artificially hasten deterioration by neglecting to do something that needs to be done. For example, natural deterioration occurs even when people add the right amount of the right lubricant at the appropriate locations and intervals. That deterioration is hastened, however, if not enough lubricant is added or if lubrication intervals are too long. This sort of neglect shortens the natural life span of the equipment.

The Buck Stops Here

To eliminate breakdowns, we must first change the idea that making products and preventing failures are two separate jobs. Preventing breakdowns depends most of all on us—the operators who are always in contact with the machines. We know and can feel the condition of equipment better than anyone else.

Achieving zero breakdowns is not just a job for maintenance people. After all, who benefits from avoiding downtime? Zero breakdowns help operators meet standards of production volume, quality, and delivery time, and that ends up benefiting everyone. We need a strong sense of mission—a sense that breakdowns are everyone's problem and everyone should have a part in avoiding them.

If you don't spot the seeds of breakdowns early, they'll grow like weeds!

Watch for Slight Abnormalities

49

Why do breakdowns happen? It's because we don't notice or watch for slight problems or abnormal conditions—the seeds that grow into breakdowns. Minor problems are defects waiting to happen.

Slight abnormalities include dirt, grime, small amounts of wear, scratches, play, looseness, leaks, corrosion, deformation, cracks, vibration, and excess heat. Most of these are small annoyances we let slip by. They are exactly the kinds of problems, however, that grow into minor stoppages or defects and eventually into total breakdowns. That is why it is essential not to overlook any problem—no matter how small.

Provide the basics

Lubricate

Tighten bolts

Clean

Stick to the rules

Work instructions

Standards

Restore deterioration

Raise skills for operating and maintaining machines

Coming to Grips with Zero Breakdowns

Four activities are fundamental to achieving zero breakdowns:

1. Provide the basics through daily checks (cleaning, lubricating and tightening)

2. Stick to the rules (use and operate machines correctly)

3. Restore deterioration (eliminate or control factors that cause deterioration

4. Sharpen operations and maintenance skills

Pursuing these four strategies lets operators perform their daily work with greater confidence and efficiency.

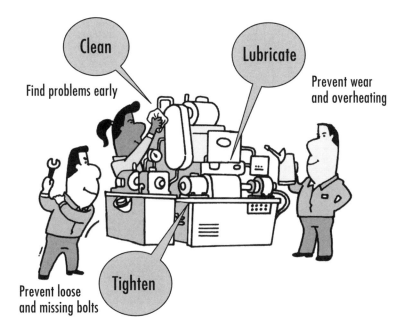

Clean — Find problems early

Lubricate — Prevent wear and overheating

Tighten — Prevent loose and missing bolts

Providing the Basics (Cleaning and Inspecting, Lubricating, and Tightening)

As operators, the first thing we need to do with our machines is to maintain the basic conditions for normal operation through cleaning and inspecting, lubricating, and tightening.

- *Cleaning and inspecting* keeps dirt and grime off equipment and exposes slight defects. As we clean, we touch the equipment, checking it and discovering problems.

- *Lubrication* prevents wear and overheating of sliding and rotating parts. Too often, equipment wears out early from accelerated deterioration due to improper lubrication.

- *Tightening* basic machine components like nuts and bolts is the third part of providing basic conditions. Missing or loose bolts cause excessive vibration, which leads to many machine break downs. Checking for looseness and proper tightening should become part of every operator's daily check.

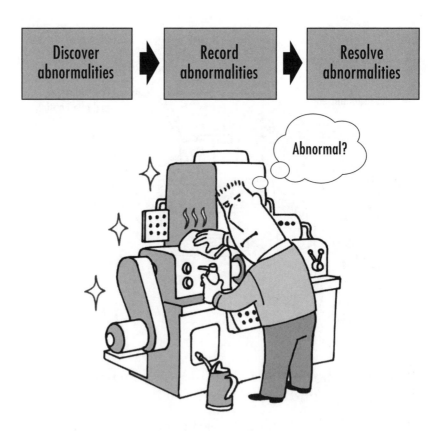

Daily Checks Are the First Step of TPM

Daily checks refers to everything equipment users do to maintain the machine: lubricating, cleaning, inspecting, tightening bolts, and so on. The operator's daily checks are the first step of TPM. These tasks are critical to ensuring that equipment doesn't break down during operation. Each workplace needs to develop a daily checklist that sets out items to be checked and actions to be taken.

Stay alert. Whenever you notice anything out of the ordinary—a peculiar noise, overheated bearings, or unusual vibrations or odors, for example—make a note of the abnormality and take the actions designated on the daily checklist.

Find the Root Cause and Restore the Equipment

53

Shopfloor employees sometimes complain that even constant restorative activities fail to reduce the number of equipment breakdowns. For example, an operator discovers that a V-belt is about to break and changes it, thinking that she has restored the machine to its proper condition. A short while later, however, the new belt wears and breaks before the end of its normal life.

The problem here is why the belt is so worn that it needs to be changed. Rather than a simple question of belt life, it may be that an off-center pulley is causing excessive wear on one side of the belt. Another possibility is that chips or dust are getting into the belt mechanism and accelerating the wear on the belt.

Asking why and getting to the heart of the root cause in this way is absolutely crucial. Unthinking parts replacement doesn't really restore the machine and all but guarantees a recurrence of the problem.

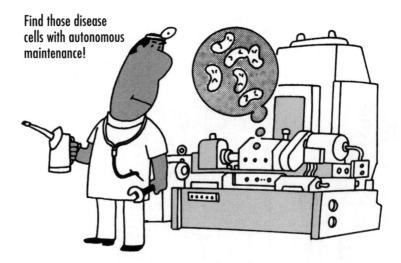

Find those disease cells with autonomous maintenance!

Nip Breakdowns in the Bud with Autonomous Maintenance

Equipment breakdowns hit operators harder than anything else—they are the biggest problems we face. This is why, during production, we need to watch for problems that might eventually grow into breakdowns. If we do this only superficially, nearly invisible defects will cluster like diseased cells and eventually bring about fatal breakdowns.

In autonomous maintenance (a characteristic TPM activity explained in Chapter 4), operators take part in preventing the deterioration that can lead to equipment breakdowns. In Step 1 of autonomous maintenance (initial cleaning), operators begin by relentlessly identifying and fixing problems. They then move on to making equipment improvements. In Step 4 (general inspection), operators learn how to make regular and thorough checks of each element of the equipment for problems that need to be corrected.

We all work together to carry out general inspections.

For each component:

- Is it being used correctly?
- Is it functioning properly?
- Are there any problems?

Why General Inspection?

55

General inspection—the fourth step of autonomous maintenance—is a vital activity for preventing equipment breakdowns.

In a general or comprehensive inspection, operators, maintenance people, designers, staff specialists, and everyone else involved with the equipment all contribute to learning and teaching the correct condition and function of each equipment component. This training helps everyone understand what constitutes normal equipment functioning and reveals any problems.

Once you understand how to conduct checks, you can confidently maintain a machine in proper condition.

Learning How Not to Break Equipment

Learning how to avoid breaking equipment involves developing knowledge and skills in five areas:

1. *Be able to spot abnormalities.*

   • Carry out daily checks reliably and judge correctly when things are abnormal

   • Understand the structure and function (i.e., operation) of the equipment

   • Use the five senses to catch abnormalities while the equipment is running

2. *Repair and restore.*

   • Improve machine operation to make it easier

   • Correct problems and restore equipment (observing and practicing simple repairs with maintenance people)

3. *Set criteria.* This means being able to draw up, apply, and teach inspection criteria.

4. *Keep equipment running.* This means knowing how to operate equipment properly.

5. *Track down causes.*

Learning from Breakdowns

When a machine breaks down, maintenance people too often do both the fixing and the analysis of causes and people on the shop floor don't even try to understand what happened. This approach doesn't help operators learn to take care of their own equipment.

To eliminate breakdowns entirely, we need to learn from each breakdown how to prevent the same failure in the future by tracking down root causes. In addition to asking "What ran out?" and "What failed?" we should ask "Why did it fail?" and "Why didn't we detect signs of failure early?" We need to ask "why" repeatedly to prevent the problem from arising again on the same machine or similar machines.

CHAPTER SUMMARY

Two types of breakdown can occur in equipment. In a *function-loss (sporadic) breakdown* the machine loses function completely. In a *function-reduction breakdown* there is a partial loss of function, resulting in defects, minor stoppages, or reduced speed.

The biggest cause of breakdowns is *human neglect*. Machines have a large number of parts that need to function properly. People cause breakdowns indirectly by misoperating equipment or forgetting to do basic maintenance like lubricating and tightening bolts.

Breakdowns happen for different reasons at different times in the equipment life cycle. Breakdowns in new equipment happen due to errors in design, fabrication, or installation. After this period is a period when breakdowns happen for unforeseeable reasons. As the machine ages, wear-related breakdowns occur due to wear and tear and deterioration.

Some equipment deterioration is natural, but in many cases our neglect leads to *accelerated deterioration*. We need to recognize that preventing breakdowns depends largely on operators—the people who are closest to the machines. Operators can sense the condition of equipment better than anyone else. And operators have the most to gain by avoiding downtime. Zero breakdowns helps us meet standards of production volume, quality, and delivery time.

Four activities are fundamental to achieving zero breakdowns:

1. Provide the basics through daily checks (cleaning, lubricating, and tightening)

59

2. Stick to the rules (use and operate machines correctly)

3. Restore deterioration (find the root causes of deterioration and eliminate or control them)

4. Sharpen operations and maintenance skills

Through *autonomous maintenance* (a series of TPM activities explained in Chapter 4), operators take part in preventing the deterioration that can lead to breakdowns.

In Step 1 of autonomous maintenance (initial cleaning), operators begin by relentlessly identifying and fixing problems. They then move on to making equipment improvements and restoring deterioration. In Step 4 (general inspection), operators review equipment conditions and functions alongside maintenance people, designers, and anyone else involved with the equipment. Through this event we learn how to regularly and thoroughly check each equipment element for problems that need to be corrected.

Autonomous Maintenance

CHAPTER 4

CHAPTER OVERVIEW

Autonomous Maintenance

- What Is Autonomous Maintenance?

- Autonomous Maintenance Step by Step

- Step 1: Clean and Inspect

- Step 2: Eliminate Problem Sources and Inaccessible Areas

- Step 3: Draw up Cleaning and Lubrication Standards

- Step 4: Conduct General Inspections

- Step 5: Conduct Autonomous Inspections

- Steps 6 and 7: Sustain Your Gains and Continue to Improve

- Why Autonomous Maintenance?

- Step Audits Are for Training and Mutual Learning

- Tags Are Bandages for Machines

- Autonomous Maintenance Is a Daily Workout for Equipment

- Who Benefits from Autonomous Maintenance?

- Summary

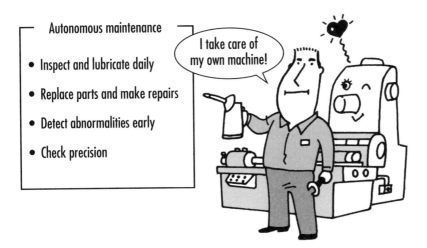

What Is Autonomous Maintenance?

The word *autonomous* means "independent." *Autonomous maintenance* refers to activities designed to involve operators in maintaining their own equipment, independent of the maintenance department. Typical activities include:

- daily inspections
- lubrication
- parts replacement
- simple repairs
- abnormality detection
- precision checks

Traditionally, production shops operated under the assumption that anything related to machines—even the most basic equipment care—was the maintenance department's responsibility.

But that approach can't get rid of breakdowns and defects. TPM gradually eliminates breakdowns and defects by training equipment operators to play a central role preventive maintenance by carrying out autonomous maintenance on a daily basis.

63

Autonomous Maintenance Step by Step

It's one thing to say that caring for equipment is part of the operator's job—but that doesn't tell us what to do or how much to do it. Autonomous maintenance is implemented in seven steps that build the skills operators need and define what they are expected to do. Managers audit each step and when the audit is satisfactory, the team moves on to the next step.

The first three steps are activities to keep the state of the equipment from deteriorating. This involves reestablishing the basic conditions for operation every day by cleaning, lubrication, and the tightening bolts and screws.

Steps 4 and 5 add general inspection standards that complement the cleaning and lubrication standards set up in Steps 1 through 3. From preventing deterioration, we move to measuring or monitoring deterioration and to developing efficient maintenance activities.

The first 5 steps of autonomous maintenance focus on the "hard," mechanical aspects of equipment maintenance. In Step 6 we concentrate on "softer" issues: straightening up, putting things in order, standardizing, and visually managing maintenance activities.

Step 7 is the beginning of truly autonomous activities. This is the stage where teams carry out maintenance activities independently and where TPM really becomes business as usual.

The Seven Steps of Autonomous Maintenance

Step	Name	Activities
1	Clean and inspect	Eliminate all dirt and grime on the machine, lubricate, tighten bolts, and find and correct problems.
2	Eliminate problem sources and inaccessible areas	Correct sources of dirt and grime; prevent spattering and improve accessibility for cleaning and lubrication. Shorten the time it takes to clean and lubricate.
3	Draw up cleaning and lubricating standards	Write standards that will ensure that cleaning, lubricating, and tightening can be done efficiently. (Make a schedule for periodic tasks.)
4	Conduct general inspections	Conduct skills training with inspection manuals and use general inspections to find and correct slight abnormalities in the equipment.
5	Conduct autonomous inspections	Prepare standard checksheets for autonomous inspections. Carry out the inspections.
6	Carry out visual maintenance management	Standardize and visually manage all shopfloor maintenance routines. Build a comprehensive system of maintenance management. Examples of standards needed: • cleaning, lubrication, and inspection standards • shopfloor materials flow standards • data recording method standards • tool and die management standards
7	Carry out consistent autonomous management	Develop company policies and objectives; make improvement activities part of everyday practice; keep reliable MTBF (mean time between failures) data, analyze it, and use it to improve equipment.

65

Cleaning is inspecting

Step 1: Clean and Inspect

Cleaning and inspecting (introduced in Chapter 3) marks the crucial start of autonomous maintenance activities. There are three main things to remember about cleaning and inspecting:

> • Cleaning is inspection
>
> • Inspecting means finding problems
>
> • Problems call for either restoration or improvement

Most people consider cleaning a nice idea, but not essential. This shows that we don't understand the real significance of cleaning.

Cleaning doesn't simply mean polishing the outside of a machine or its electrical panels or covers; it means getting rid of the years of grime coating every part of the machine. We need to take the machine off line, remove covers and guards, drain the oil tanks, and manually clean out the nooks and crannies we may never have touched before.

This sort of cleaning does more than help us find out what is wrong with equipment. It encourages us to think about what condition the machine was in when it was new—and what condition it ought to be in. Cleaning activity that doesn't expose what's wrong with equipment is no more than polishing and buffing; it misses the point that cleaning is inspection.

Thoroughly cleaning a piece of equipment will reveal many conditions that aren't as they should be. This is why we say that cleaning cannot be separated from inspecting for deviations from the normal or proper state of the equipment. Whenever we find such a deviation, we mark it with a red tag.

Red-tagging

• Attach tags to problems revealed by cleaning/inspecting

• Fix the problems right away. Then remove the tags

• For a problem that can't be fixed immediately, draw up a clear plan to remove the tag

67

Step 2: Eliminate Problem Sources and Inaccessible Areas

It's hard work to get rid of years of grime, but when you're done, you feel much closer to the machine. You also spot problems you hadn't seen before. Here are some common situations:

- Some machines get dirty soon after cleaning no matter how often you clean them. And you wonder whether there isn't some way to avoid having to clean them all the time. You're right, of course. Machines will slip back to the way they were before cleaning unless you control the source of the contamination.

- You understand the need for cleaning/inspecting and lubricating, but they take too long because some areas are difficult to reach. Isn't there some way to cut the time it takes to do all that? Right again—if areas that need cleaning or lubricating are hard to get to, then we need to make them more accessible.

In Step 2, we use this natural interest and desire to make Step 1 tasks easier to create tangible results. We learn how to keep equipment from deteriorating and establish the basic conditions for easy machine maintenance.

Problem Sources and Inaccessible Areas

- Stop contamination at the source

- Minimize (localize) contamination

- Modify equipment to make cleaning and lubrication easier

- Install covers and inspection windows to make checking easier

---

Problem Sources and Inaccessible Areas

Stop contamination
at the source!

Minimize contamination

Modify equipment to make cleaning easier

Install covers and inspection
windows to make checking easier

Develop the ability to make standards!

Step 3: Draw Up Cleaning and Lubrication Standards

The purpose of maintenance is to maintain equipment or machinery in its ideal or optimal state. The important activities we carry out in Step 2 are designed to facilitate maintenance of basic equipment conditions—those relating to cleaning, inspecting, lubricating, and tightening. These activities prevent deterioration.

In Step 3 team members decide what standards they need to follow to prevent deterioration of their equipment. These can't be standards that managers or technicians force onto shopfloor people. As operators, we need to understand the rules we are supposed to follow—and the reason for those rules. Based on that understanding, we learn how to set standards for ourselves that are realistic as well as effective.

Learn structures and functions

Actually inspect

Fix problems

A new problem!

Establish visual controls

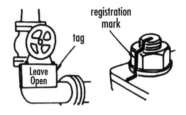

Step 4: Conduct General Inspections

The first three steps of autonomous maintenance made us more familiar with our equipment. In Step 4, general inspection, we acquire machine-related knowledge and troubleshooting skills to supplement our five senses and the abilities we have already developed for finding problems. After learning more about the equipment structure and functions, we establish tentative standards and thoroughly reinspect our machines based on this new knowledge.

Key Step 4 Activities

1. Learn the structure and functions of your own equipment (training by leader)

2. Test your understanding and then actually inspect the equipment

3. Correct new problems you find

4. Establish thorough visual controls to help control equipment conditions

Coordinate activities by the end of Step 5

Step 5: Conduct Autonomous Inspections

In Step 5 of autonomous maintenance, we revise the cleaning, inspection, and lubrication standards developed in Steps 1 through 3, as well as the tentative inspection standards we developed for each general inspection item in Step 4. We streamline those tasks to ensure that we can carry out maintenance reliably within the time allotted.

At this stage we decide what combination of specialized maintenance tasks and autonomous maintenance activities will create the most efficient system overall. This means integrating and consolidating autonomous maintenance tasks and standards within the maintenance department's annual maintenance calendar and major servicing standards (specific standards for checks, inspections, replacements, and overhauls requiring disassembly).

Visual Maintenance Controls

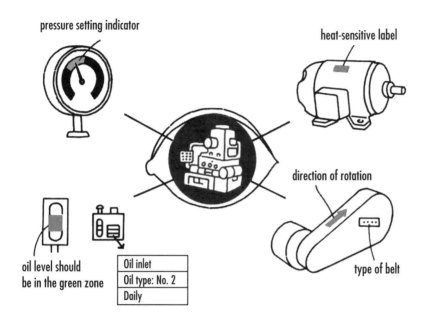

Steps 6 and 7: Sustain Your Gains and Continue to Improve

The sixth step of autonomous maintenance is often called "maintenance management," but what it really means is *standardization* with a special focus on visual management. The aim here is to sort out and properly arrange objects in the workplace, defining procedures that need to be followed, performing equipment precision checks, and facilitating operator tasks.

Standardization also includes applying all kinds of improvements and ingenuity to organize raw materials, work-in-process, tools, maintenance supplies, and so on, that need to be managed, creating your own standards, learning the skills needed to follow procedures correctly, and relentlessly applying the principles of visual management. All these activities are completed in Step 6. The final step, Step 7, confirms autonomous maintenance through regular practice, ensuring that activities continue. It also supports further equipment improvement through accurate record-keeping of mean time between failure (MTBF) and other key measures.

74

Why Autonomous Maintenance?

"Sure, more work for me!" Many operators react this way when they see what is involved and realize that autonomous maintenance is the operator's job.

Ideally equipment maintenance should be carried out by the operator, and that used to be common practice. After the idea of preventive maintenance was introduced, jobs became more specialized. Some people operated machines and others maintained and fixed them.

We began to understand the need to return to the traditional approach through autonomous maintenance when we realized that relying solely on maintenance people doesn't really allow us to reduce breakdowns and quality rejects.

A step audit provides both guidance and mutual learning.

Step Audits for Training and Mutual Learning

At each autonomous maintenance step, shopfloor managers conduct an audit to see how the teams are doing. Step audits are not about managers passing judgment on the people who work for them. They are chances for people on the shop floor to learn what the boss thinks and expects—and for the boss to recognize the hard work shopfloor people have done and to gain a better understanding of current problems.

For both managers and operators, a step audit is a golden opportunity to confront the reality of their workplace, to think about where they are headed and to discuss what needs to be done now.

Autonomous maintenance step audits provide a forum for people giving and receiving advice to learn from one another and to grow together. Be prepared to repeat important points over and over again and to be thorough in your evaluation.

75

Tags Are Bandages for Machines

We explained on page 67 how to use tags to make equipment problems visible. What is important is not simply attaching tags but removing them. A piece of equipment covered with tags is like a sick person covered with bandages—the pain is still there. All that has changed is that defects that used to be hidden are now visible. To change the situation, we need to systematically eliminate the problems we brought to the surface.

Tags are tools for spotlighting how bad the workplace is, and as such they can be used everywhere in the workplace—not only on machines. The key point about tagging is that, from the cleaning stage onward, tags make it clear which areas on the shop floor need improvement.

Autonomous Maintenance Is a Daily Workout for Equipment

77

Breakdowns, minor stoppages, and other problems decrease when autonomous maintenance takes hold and we can clearly see the actual condition of the workplace and improve it. But some problems are so big that operators can't do anything about them on their own. Such situations call for more ambitious measures from the plant maintenance staff.

Big improvements of this type usually show results right away, but conditions can still slip back to the way they were fairly quickly. Doing autonomous maintenance, on the other hand, is like doing regular exercise. Small improvements slowly but surely build strength. In the workplace, these small improvements build a system that makes it possible to sustain results. Constant strength-building and conditioning activities are as important for equipment as they are for people.

- Proud of my company
- Proud of myself
- Proud of my equipment

78

Who Benefits from Autonomous Maintenance?

A goal of autonomous maintenance is for everyone in the workplace to work effectively and healthily. But when everything is covered with dirt and grime, people can't take pride in their company, their jobs or themselves.

In a workplace constantly harassed by breakdowns, defects, or minor stoppages, people end up forgetting what their jobs are supposed to be. They can only do the work they are supposed to do when the equipment does what it is designed to do.

The point is clear. You don't practice autonomous maintenance just to improve the equipment or your company—you do it to make your own work easier.

CHAPTER SUMMARY

The word *autonomous* means "independent." *Autonomous maintenance* refers to activities designed to involve operators in maintaining their own equipment, independent of the maintenance department. Typical activities include:

- daily inspections
- simple repairs
- lubrication
- abnormality detection
- parts replacement
- precision checks

Autonomous maintenance is implemented in *seven steps* that build the skills operators need and define what they are expected to do:

1. Clean and inspect

2. Eliminate problem sources and inaccessible areas

3. Draw up cleaning and lubrication standards

4. Conduct general inspections

5. Conduct autonomous inspections

6 and 7. Sustain your gains and continue to improve

Steps 1, 2, and 3 are activities to keep the state of the equipment from deteriorating. This involves *reestablishing the basic conditions* for daily operation by cleaning, lubricating, and tightening bolts and screws. This is a deep cleaning that involves taking the equipment off line, removing grime, and exposing areas we may never have touched before. *Cleaning is inspection.* It encourages us to think about what condition the machine was in when it was new—and what condition it ought to be in now.

Steps 4 and 5 add *general inspection standards* that complement the cleaning and lubrication standards set up in Steps 1 through 3. From preventing deterioration, we move to measuring or monitoring deterioration and to developing efficient maintenance activities.

The first five steps of autonomous maintenance focus on the "hard," mechanical aspects of equipment maintenance. In Step 6 we concentrate on "softer" issues: straightening up, putting things in order, standardizing, and visually managing maintenance activities.

Step 7 is the beginning of truly autonomous activities. This is the stage where teams carry out maintenance activities independently and where TPM really becomes a standard part of daily activities.

As the TPM team masters each step, it reviews its accomplishments with managers in a step audit.

During autonomous maintenance operators sometimes attach tags to equipment problems to make them more visible. What is important is not how these tags are put on, but how they are removed as problems are resolved at the source.

Autonomous maintenance is like a daily workout for equipment. Through small improvements, the workplace becomes a strong system that can sustain results.

Team Activities

CHAPTER 5

CHAPTER OVERVIEW

Team Activities

- What Are TPM Team Activities
- Goals of Team Activities
- Selecting Leaders
- The Team Leader: A Crucial Role
- Team Members Are Important, Too
- How to Choose a Project
- Set Firm Objectives
- Involve Management in Auditing Team Activities
- Three Secret Weapons for Teams
- Using Activity Boards Effectively
- How to Hold Productive Meetings
- Using One-Point Lessons
- Publicize Results
- Summary

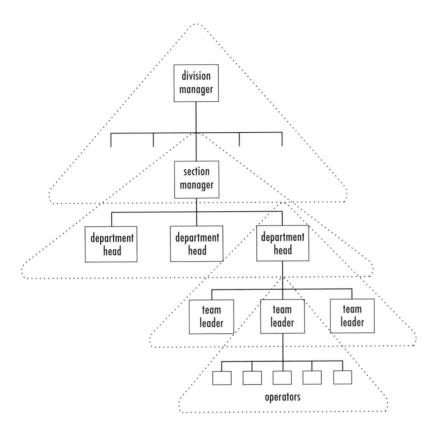

What Are TPM Team Activities?

Team activities are basic to TPM. Major results come when everyone participates, from the chief executive to frontline operators. In TPM, we form different teams at different levels: top management teams, middle management teams, and shopfloor teams. Each one has its own objectives and its own part to play. Each has its own challenges and successes.

The leader of a team at one level is a member of a team at the next higher level. These leaders act as liaisons between the teams and assure close communication horizontally and vertically throughout the organization. This arrangement is called "overlapping teams."

Let's look at how shopfloor teams work.

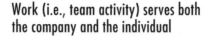

Work (i.e., team activity) serves both
the company and the individual

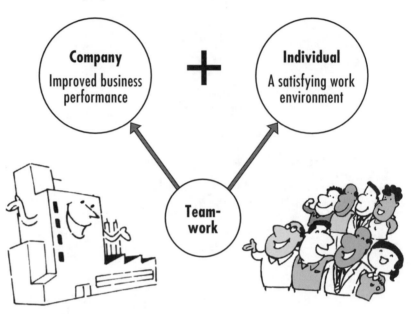

Goals of Team Activities

TPM promotes team activities that work hand in hand with management activities. Localized team activities, in other words, have the same goals as the plantwide TPM program.

What are the goals of TPM? The first is to eradicate the six big losses: breakdowns, lengthy changeovers and adjustments, minor stoppages, speed reductions, defects and rework, and yield losses. Eliminating these losses aims at maximizing overall equipment effectiveness, achieving production schedules, honoring delivery commitments, preserving and improving quality, lowering costs, and maintaining a safe (and pollution-free) environment. The purpose of each of these measures is twofold: to increase company profits at the same time as we create a more satisfying workplace.

To put it another way, autonomous maintenance is inseparable from our work and it is through teams that we carry out autonomous maintenance.

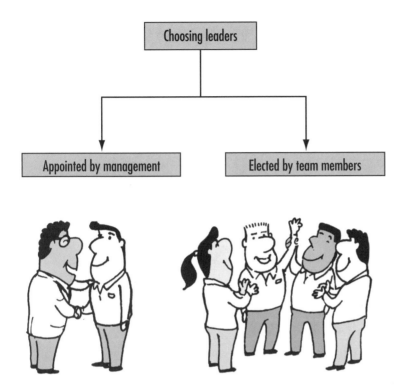

Selecting Leaders

Since TPM team activities are part of the everyday business of the company, team leaders are typically the people whose job it is to carry out management instructions and directives. In some companies this means that supervisors lead the TPM teams. In other companies, workteam members elect their own leaders and management provides backup support.

People who serve as team leaders need more than just specialized technical knowledge, quality awareness, and a grasp of improvement techniques. They also must have strong leadership and facilitation skills to support and motivate the entire group.

Leadership will determine whether we succeed or not.

The Team Leader: A Crucial Role

The leader's job is to steer a particular activity efficiently in a limited period of time. To organize and energize the team, a leader needs to pay attention to the following:

1. Guide the team by continually linking team activities to workplace priorities. Get help from managers and supervisors.

2. Work to get everyone involved and to build good relationships among team members.

3. Keep in contact with other teams to share ideas.

4. Take the lead in learning new techniques and coach team members in their use.

Team Members Are Important, Too

Leaders can't do everything by themselves. Meaningful results come when everyone participates. Aside from sharing the team experience, each team member needs to take on and carry out individual assignments. Here are some examples of team member roles and responsibilities:

1. Take part in team activities and share your ideas and opinions at meetings.

2. Carry out special assignments.

3. Learn techniques, methods, and skills you need to participate in improvement activities.

4. Work for smooth personal relationships between team members.

The team experience will benefit you most when you take an active role—don't just watch from the sidelines.

| Plant manager | ---- | Annual goal | ---- | 10% increase in OEE |

| Section head | ---- | Annual goal | ---- | Cut downtime due to breakdowns by half |

| Team leader | ---- | Project theme | ---- | Choose themes and targets that correspond to management goals |

Team — Reduce sporadic breakdowns

How to Choose a Project

The results your team gets will depend largely on how you choose your project. Don't choose a project casually or by intuition. Hold a team meeting and discuss what needs to be done and what the current priorities are. You need to consider problems from a broad perspective. To make these discussions effective, use an *activities board* to record shopfloor conditions.

When selecting a project, listen carefully to the managers' priorities and understand what they expect of the team. List the problems that affect your workplace and begin by tackling the one that is most likely to help achieve plantwide or area goals.

Theme: Sporadic breakdown reduction

No. of breakdowns

Target item

No. of breakdowns on Machine X

Current: 10 per month

In six months: 5 per month

Numerical target

Month

Project duration

Set Firm Objectives

For effective activities, you need to build a team of people with a shared perspective, working toward shared goals.

Team activities can't go smoothly if you haven't clarified and agreed on the goals and objectives. Once you have selected a project theme, you need to get everyone on the same track by making specific decisions about What (objectives), When (the duration of activities) and How (numerical targets). Decide exactly how far the team should go and set concrete targets. This will make it easier to see whether or not you have been successful. Once you have clear targets, you will be able to evaluate your results and plan your next activities more easily.

- I see what management is driving at.

- I understand what sort of problems the teams are running into.

- This makes evaluations and corrections easier and will speed up the improvement process.

Involve Management in Auditing Team Activities

The person in charge of TPM programs in the company serves as a coach for the shopfloor teams and keeps team activities energized and on track. In addition, managers are asked to conduct periodic reviews of team activities.

Having supervisors or managers guide team activities through the audits or checks clarifies management policies and priorities, boosts team member motivation, and helps ensure satisfying activities.

Management audits identify any problems with what the team is doing and make it easy to evaluate activities and adjust course if necessary. This input keeps team activities moving ahead.

- Activity boards
- Meetings
- One-point lessons

91

Three Secret Weapons for Teams

The key to successful team activities is to make sure the team members are motivated and capable, and have opportunities to make a difference. Each team member needs to develop his or her own attitudes, knowledge, and skill.

For the team as a whole, there are three "secret weapons" that lead to success:

- activity boards
- meetings
- one-point lessons

Using Activity Boards Effectively

An activity board is more than just a bulletin board for posting results and communicating team information. It is a tool that links company goals with things the teams need to do, problems occurring in the workplace, and how the teams are trying to solve them.

In keeping with this broader purpose of an activity board, it should contain items like the ones listed in the table below. The important thing is that the team, maintenance staff, and the managers can clearly see what is being recorded, what the team has been doing, where things stand, and what challenges lie ahead.

An activity board is like a scoreboard for the workplace. It should be set up in the team meeting space and should be the basis for the group's discussion. The illustration on the opposite page shows a sample activity board.

92

Activity Board Items

1. Corporate vision
   - Objectives
   - Policy

2. Progress chart
   - Plan
   - Progress

3. Records
   - Equipment effectiveness

4. Remaining issues
   - Focused improvements
   - Autonomous maintenance

5. Evaluation

6. One-point lessons

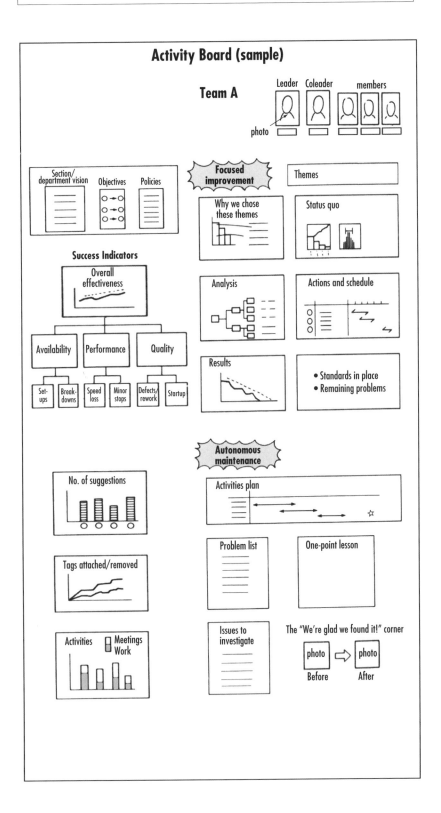

Activity Board (sample)

Team A

Leader   Coleader   members

photo

Section/department vision   Objectives   Policies

Focused improvement

Themes

Why we chose these themes

Status quo

Success Indicators

Overall effectiveness

Analysis

Actions and schedule

Availability   Performance   Quality

Set-ups   Break-downs   Speed loss   Minor stops   Defects/rework   Startup

Results

• Standards in place
• Remaining problems

Autonomous maintenance

No. of suggestions

Activities plan

Tags attached/removed

Problem list

One-point lesson

Activities   Meetings Work

Issues to investigate

The "We're glad we found it!" corner

photo   ⇨   photo

Before   After

How to Hold Productive Meetings

Team activities get their energy from group meetings in which everyone participates. Compared to the ideas an individual employee might come up with, the improvement suggestions that come out of team discussions are often more varied and of higher quality. Talking together also sharpens problem awareness and helps develop shared ways of seeing problems.

Team leadership has a big effect on the quality of team activities. The leader has to be able to integrate every member's ideas and opinions. Meetings should be short and frequent, and the leader should make sure the time is spent well by setting an agenda beforehand. Typical agenda items include:

- progress toward goals

- problem areas

- improvement action plans

- expected results

After every team meeting the leader should inform management of the issues discussed, conclusions reached, and plans for the next meeting. Summarizing a meeting is a good way to reflect on what was said and clarify what to discuss the next time. Meeting reports help managers understand issues the team is facing and allows them to offer appropriate guidance and support. This is a major source of energy for team activities. A sample meeting summary is illustrated on the opposite page.

Team Activity Report (Sample)

Team report	Issued	10 Oct 19•• (No. 5)		
	Team name	The Defect Detectives		
Theme	Unit	Machining Sec. 3/Group 1/Squad 5		
Preparing for Step 2 audit	Team leader	Sue M.	**Secretary**	Joe B.
	Activity Content			
	Work hours	__:__ to __:__		
Members	Meetings	4:00 p.m. to 5:00 p.m.		
Sue M., Jerry L., Joe B., Tony O., Dan S., Ellen B.	Training	Month/day/__:__ to __:__		
Absent none	Total time	(1 hour) x (6 people) = (6 hours)		

Items	Actions and Implementations	When	Who
The Step 2 assessment will take place on 10/22. What do we need to do before then?	(1) Review initial cleaning (day/ night shifts) /conduct intensive 15-minute cleaning after breaks.	From 10/8	All
	(2) Identify major issues from initial cleaning.		JB
	(3) On activity board, record number of oil leak tags removed.		JL
Antispatter cover installed, but leakage still occurs through gaps around cover.	Try no. 8 local cover.		SM TO
Verify phenomenon.	Record with camcorder.		DS EB

Section Head Remarks	Improvement Coordinator Remarks	Group Leader Remarks
Study Step 3 materials.	Meet more often.	Stick with the PDCA cycle.

95

Using One-Point Lessons

Team leaders (or supervisors) who have been trained in the TPM basics, should turn around and train their team members. But it is important that they not just teach the same thing they were taught. Leaders need to adapt the principles they have learned to their own workplace. This process helps them learn and teaching reinforces their leadership role.

One effective tool for teaching is the short, focused "one-point lesson," which addresses a single topic on one sheet of paper and can be covered in about 10 minutes.

One-point lessons come in three types, depending on their purpose:

1. *Basic Lessons*—These describe something team members need to know for everyday production work or participation in TPM activities.

2. *Problem Case Studies*—These use actual examples of breakdowns, defects, and so on, to illustrate what should be done every day to prevent problems from recurring.

3. *Improvement Case Studies*—These describe the concepts, contents, and results of actual improvements made on the shop floor during team activities so that similar improvements can be made in other areas.

Even after training other team members, the leader needs to make sure (through repeated training) that everyone understands the lesson and that what was learned is being put into practice.

Leaders need to stay alert to any aspect of improvement activities that team members are struggling with.

One-Point Lesson:
Hydraulic Power Unit Inspection

Purpose of Inspection

The hydraulic power unit provides power to the entire hydraulic system. Even if you use the right amount of oil, local oil shortages, clogged filters, or other causes may result in cavitation.*

This can cause problems (noise, corrosion, pressure fluctuations, or vibration) in hydraulic devices throughout the system, so daily checks are essential.

What to Check and How

Daily checks can be performed during operation and consist of looking for abnormalities using temperature and other gauges, as well as the human senses of sight, hearing, and touch.

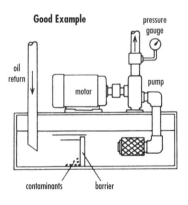

Bad Example

pressure gauge

oil return

pump

motor

oil level gauge

suction filter

Good Example

pressure gauge

oil return

pump

motor

contaminants   barrier

Reprinted courtesy of Zexel Corp.

1. Check Oil Volume

When the oil drops below the lower indicator line of the oil volume gauge, the suction filter pulls in air and air enters the return tube. Add oil when this occurs.

2. Check Suction Filter

A clogged suction filter causes air to enter the system. Remove the filter to check. If contamination is light, wash with detergent oil and replace the filter. Replace the filter if contamination is heavy. Consider using a barrier to keep contaminants away from the oil intake.

3. Check Suction Joints, Gaskets, and Pipes

Tighten any loose joints. Replace any deteriorated gaskets. Check for hairline cracks in pipes and repair or replace if any are found.

* When a local drop in oil pressure occurs, dissolved air escapes in the form of bubbles. When rapid pressure is then applied, the air has no time to redissolve and the air becomes supercompressed and causes noise as it strikes a surface. This is called cavitation.

Presenter — A presentation is a chance for both to learn. → Audience

Decline in Major Breakdowns

- What methods and techniques did you use?
- What knowhow did you need?
- What problems did you run into?

98

Publicize Results

Presenting a summary of what you did and what results you obtained is the final wrap-up to a team activity. Presentations are helpful in a couple of ways. People will do work they will be proud of when they know they will have to give a public report. At the same time, putting together an account of team activities provides both a good opportunity for reflection and a good starting point for future activities.

Presenting is an approach for mutual learning. The presentation session is a forum in which for presenters and their audience can learn together. Teams trade vivid stories about how they applied various techniques, what they learned and what struggles they faced. These stories lead to questions from the audience and to improved ideas that everyone present can discuss. This interaction is one of the most important aspects of a presentation. The emcee at a presentation session needs to make sure that the talking is not all one-way.

CHAPTER SUMMARY

Team activities are basic to TPM. TPM activities are carried out by teams at the top management, middle management, and shopfloor levels. Each type of team has its own objectives and part to play.

TPM uses *overlapping teams*—the leader of a team at one level is a member of a team at the next level. These leaders act as liaisons between the teams and assure close communication throughout the company.

Shopfloor TPM team activities have the same goals as the plantwide TPM program: to get rid of the six big losses. Achieving this enables the company to maximize overall equipment effectiveness (OEE), meet production schedules, honor delivery commitments, improve quality, lower costs, and maintain a safe environment. Through TPM we increase company profits at the same time as we create a more satisfying workplace.

Since TPM is an integral element of company management, frontline supervisors lead the TPM teams in some companies. In other companies, teams elect their own leaders and management provides backup support. The *team leader* guides group activities and keeps everyone involved and working well together. He or she stays in touch with other teams to share ideas, and takes the lead in learning and teaching new techniques.

TPM *team members* are no less important. Team members participate in team activities and share ideas and opinions. They learn and apply new techniques and skills to implement improvements. The team experience will benefit you most when you take an active role.

99

Teams should choose projects that address current management priorities and targets. List the problems that affect your workplace and tackle the one most likely to help achieve plantwide or area goals. Set clear objectives—What, When, and How—so you can see whether you have been successful.

Three secret weapons support effective TPM teamwork, motivation, and skill building: activity boards, meetings, and one-point lessons.

An *activity board* is like a visual scoreboard for the workplace, linking company goals with things the teams need to do, problems in the workplace, and team efforts to solve them.

Meetings provide the energy for team activities. Improvement suggestions that come out of team discussions are often stronger than individual employee ideas. Talking together sharpens problem awareness and develops shared ways of seeing problems. Using an agenda will help team leaders make best use of everyone's time. Meeting reports help managers understand and lend support to team activities.

One-point lessons address a single topic for simple training that can be covered in about 10 minutes. Basic lessons, problem case studies, and improvement examples are the three main types.

A team project should wrap up with a presentation of results—a learning opportunity for the presenters as well as for the audience.

TPM and Safety

CHAPTER 6

CHAPTER OVERVIEW

TPM and Safety

- Safety Is the Cornerstone of Production Activities
- Drive the "Three Evils" Out of the Workplace
- Why Do Accidents Happen?
- The Pyramid of Accident Causes
- Three Safety Principles
- Develop Safety Together with Autonomous Maintenance
- Safety Activities Should Be Continual and Progressive
- Making Safety Checks
- Making Maintenance Activities Safer
- Standardizing Operations
- Checkpoints for Nonrepetitive Activities
- Hazard Awareness Training
- Active Signaling
- Three Secret Weapons for Safety Awareness
- Draw up a Safety Promotion Plan
- Summary

A workplace where we never have
to worry about safety!

Safety Is the Cornerstone of Production Activities

103

Our goal in production is to make the customer happy with attractive products, of *high quality, low cost, and speedy delivery.*

To accomplish this, production must take place in an environment where people never have to worry about injury.

When we think for a moment about why people work, we realize that not having to worry is a basic precondition for work and that safety is the cornerstone of production.

Safety is also a cornerstone of TPM. We think of safety as "maintaining peace of mind." The basic principle behind TPM safety activities is to address dangerous conditions and behavior before they cause accidents.

Three Workplace Evils

Drive the "Three Evils" Out of the Workplace

A workplace that is easy to work in must first be one where people can work without worrying. Creating such a workplace requires getting rid of the "three evils:" *difficulty, dirt,* and *danger.*

- Difficult tasks are hard to do right because they are so fatiguing.

- Dirt is more than just unsanitary. If neglected, it can cause equipment to break down and create unsafe conditions.

- Such conditions create a dangerous workplace and sooner or later will cause major accidents.

Use TPM to eliminate difficulty, dirt, and danger from the workplace and create a working environment where it is easy to work.

Unsafe condition	Unsafe behavior

Why Do Accidents Happen?

Accidents occur when unsafe conditions combine with unsafe behavior. *Unsafe conditions* are physical problems such as missing guardrails or inadequate safety devices. *Unsafe behavior* refers to actions resulting from a failure to stick to specified standards. Examples include using the wrong tools or protective gear, or ignoring signals from others when working together.

When an accident occurs, people tend to look only at the immediate cause. It is more important, though, to understand which unsafe conditions combined with which unsafe behavior and to take action to make sure it doesn't happen again.

To prevent accidents, we have to eliminate from daily practice both the unsafe conditions and the unsafe behaviors that lie at their root.

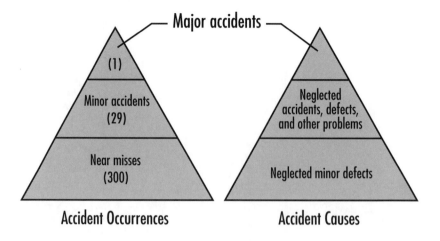

The Pyramid of Accident Causes

For every single major accident there are 29 less serious incidents and 300 near misses. This statistic is often shown graphically as a pyramid with the major accident only the narrow point at the top. The point is that things aren't necessarily safe just because a major accident hasn't occurred yet—it's just luck.

This principle tells us that, in fact, many factors in the workplace can cause major accidents. These factors are hidden in equipment and in human work procedures. They are the sort of trivial problems we overlook every day because they don't seem worth bothering with. The only way to break down the pyramid is to root out every one of these tiny problems.

The Three Principles of Safety

Workplace organization (5S)

Checks and servicing

Standardization

Work Standards

Inspection Standards

Three Safety Principles

Workplace organization and discipline, inspections and servicing, and standardization are all essential elements in creating a safe workplace. They are the three basic principles of safety.

Workplace organization and discipline are so important that many people call them "the beginning and the end" of safety. In particular, everyone needs to understand the importance of discipline and adherence to established standards. Never forget that major accidents happen when people start thinking that "someone else will take care of it," or "I'm only one person, so it doesn't matter."

The functions and performance of equipment and safety devices deteriorate with use, so it is vital to carry out regular maintenance tasks—*inspections and servicing*—as determined by law, by industry, or by in-house standards.

Finally, we need to *standardize* people's work procedures after determining correct methods and task sequences. A safe job is one that anyone can perform confidently and rapidly.

Develop Safety Together with Autonomous Maintenance

It is effective to link safety activities in TPM to the step-by-step development of autonomous maintenance. When a breakdown or minor stoppage halts a machine, for example, it is unsafe to put one's hand among machine parts that would ordinarily be moving. Unfamiliarity with equipment can also lead to unintentional misuse that can cause accidents.

Autonomous maintenance activities can improve safety in such cases by eliminating breakdowns and minor stoppages on the one hand and by standardizing human procedures and responses on the other.

Many factors cause accidents, however, and they cannot all be removed at once. In addition, many such factors are small and easy to overlook.

Safety Activities Should Be Continual and Progressive

Safety activities in the workplace need to be carried out continually and systematically.

In TPM, safety activities are a perfect match for the seven steps of autonomous maintenance. The chart on the opposite page gives tips for eliminating unsafe conditions and unsafe behavior from your workplace by integrating safety issues into autonomous maintenance activities. It is easy to make safety check items part of your equipment inspection checklists.

Safety and Autonomous Maintenance Step by Step	
1. Clean and inspect	**Eliminate unsafe conditions** • Identify and correct problems such as exposed moving parts, projecting parts, spattering of harmful substances
2. Eliminate problem sources and inaccessible areas	• Take steps to correct problems related to covers, guards, etc.
3. Draw up standards	• Establish and review work standards and daily check methods, etc.
4. Conduct general inspection	• Check and improve performance of safety and disposal devices
5. Conduct autonomous inspections	**Eliminate unsafe behavior** • Correct stressful working postures and methods
6. Carry out visual maintenance management	• Assure workplace organization (5S) and maintain a proper working environment
7. Carry out consistent autonomous management	• Encourage everyone to take care of their own workplaces

Making Safety Checks

Various forms of equipment improvement are part of both autonomous maintenance activities and the maintenance department's improvement maintenance activities.

Whatever kind of equipment maintenance activities you engage in, be sure to conduct safety checks that address the following types of issues:

1. Leaks and spattering

2. Heat

3. Equipment load

4. Reduced performance

5. Vibration and excessive noise

6. Electrical leakage and static electricity

7. Problems during operation

8. Problems during processing or execution

Questions for Safer Maintenance Activities

1. Are aisles and work locations clear?

2. Are disassembly and assembly easy?

3. Is it easy to replace broken parts?

4. Is lubrication easy? Can lubrication be centralized?

5. Do operators have the necessary knowledge and qualifications?

Making Maintenance Activities Safer

Maintenance includes a broad range of activities, from fixing sporadic breakdowns to regular inspection and servicing to implementing improvement measures for enhancing the performance or life of equipment.

For safety's sake, we need to standardize procedures to make sure we don't neglect essential issues like the following:

1. Are aisles and work areas kept clean and clear?

2. Is the equipment easy to take apart and reassemble?

3. Can machine parts be replaced easily when breakdowns occur?

4. Is the machine easy to lubricate?

5. Do the people operating the machines have the necessary knowledge and qualifications?

111

112

Standardizing Operations

Work standards are meaningless unless they are "living standards." They need to be revised to keep pace with improvements in work methods. The illustration shows examples of standardization to promote safety.

Checkpoints for Nonrepetitive Tasks

People — Assignments (who does what); coordinator; employees

Operations — Job Schedule; work methods; liaison; preparation of materials and tools

Processes — machine and equipment stoppages; down; work platform; protection of drive belts; spatters, drips, spurts; lighting; electrical hazards; hazardous materials; toxic gases, acids; open flames

113

Checkpoints for Nonrepetitive Activities

Many maintenance tasks are nonrepetitive. Any nonrepetitive task needs to begin with preparation and planning based on an adequate understanding of the equipment. The illustration shows examples of areas to develop into checkpoints for nonrepetitive tasks.

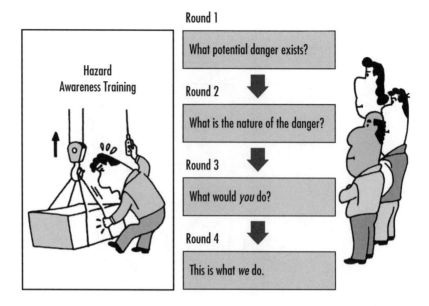

Hazard Awareness Training

The four-round hazard awareness training technique is a method that uses illustrations and photographs to train people to see and deal with potential dangers in equipment and work methods.

The method proceeds in four sequential rounds:

Round 1: What potential danger exists?

Round 2: What is the nature of the danger?

Round 3: What would *you* do?

Round 4: This is what *we* do.

Active Signaling

Most people think of unsafe behavior as the result of slightly relaxed attention, but we need to recognize that everyone makes mistakes. The more tired or distracted we are, the more apt we are to make an error. No one can stay at the peak of alertness all day long.

Many workplaces use visual and vocal signaling because it seems to be effective in preventing the kind of forgetting or goofing or other types of accidents that arise from inattention.

In signaling, workers may call out to each other or use a visual signal to indicate what they are about to do and to make sure the other person gets the message. (Many people are familiar with this in the verbal cross-checks used by workers in oil-change businesses.) The active use of signaling can drive unsafe behavior from the workplace.

Three Secret Weapons for Safety Activities

Three Secret Weapons for Safety Awareness

TPM safety awareness activities will be more effective when your team uses the three "secret weapons" mentioned earlier:

- activity boards
- one-point lessons
- meetings

Activity boards

These show the content and results of ongoing safety activities. Your team may choose to have a separate safety board or make a "safety corner" on a regular TPM activity board.

One-point lessons

Simple lessons based on actual accidents or key safety issues in daily operations can be covered in a few minutes at the start of the working day or at other times.

Make Safety Part of the Job

Hazard awareness activities

These are activities that take hazard awareness training one step further. Designed to integrate safety into the job, these activities help operators detect and eliminate dangers in everyday operations.

A safe environment through total employee involvement!

Draw up a Safety Promotion Plan

This chapter has given you an overview of safety activities in the context of TPM. Safety activities are characterized by a step-by-step progression, active signaling to prevent accidents, workplace organization, and training. Promoting safety activities requires the involvement of everyone from the chief executive to frontline operators.

Although top management's goals for safety determines the general direction of activities, the people on the shop floor are the driving force behind safety promotion. The company needs a plan to keep shopfloor activities headed in the right direction and moving forward. Each workteam should develop safety activity plans that take top management's vision and link it to specific actions the team needs to take.

CHAPTER SUMMARY

Safety is a cornerstone of TPM. We think of safety as "maintaining peace of mind." The basic principle behind TPM safety activities is to address dangerous conditions and behavior before they cause accidents.

A workplace that is easy to work in must first be one where people can work without worrying. Creating such a workplace requires using TPM to get rid of the "three evils:" *difficulty, dirt,* and *danger.*

Accidents occur when *unsafe conditions combine with unsafe behavior.* When an accident occurs, people tend to look only at the immediate cause. It is more important to understand which unsafe conditions combined with which unsafe behavior, and to take action to make sure it doesn't happen again.

For every major accident there are 29 less serious incidents and 300 near misses—remember the *accident cause pyramid.* Many factors can cause major accidents. These factors are hidden in equipment and in human work procedures. They are the sort of problems we overlook every day because they seem too trivial. The only way to break down the pyramid is to eliminate these tiny problems.

Workplace organization and discipline, regular inspections and servicing, and standardization of work procedures are the three basic principles of safety. All are essential elements in creating a safe workplace.

Autonomous maintenance promotes safety by *eliminating breakdowns and standardizing procedures and responses* to equipment situations. Eliminate unsafe conditions and unsafe behavior from your workplace by integrating safety

119

issues into autonomous maintenance activities. Make *safety check items* part of your equipment inspection checklists. Plan and coordinate *nonrepetitive maintenance tasks* to avoid safety hazards.

Hazard awareness training is a four-round approach that uses illustrations and photographs to train people to see and deal with potential dangers in equipment and work methods.

Active signaling is used to prevent errors between people working together on maintenance or other tasks. In signaling, workers may call out to each other or use a visual signal to indicate what they are about to do and to make sure the other person gets the message.

Organize safety activities in the workplace using the *three secret weapons:* activity boards, meetings, and one-point lessons.

Further Reading

T. Asaka and K. Ozeki, eds., *Handbook of Quality Tools* (Productivity Press, 1990), part II.
Gives steps and clear examples for how to use the main "QC tools" that help teams analyze and solve problems: graphs, radar charts, Pareto diagrams, cause-and-effect diagrams, tally sheets, histograms, control charts, scatter diagrams, and stratification.

M. Greif, *The Visual Factory* (Productivity Press, 1991).
Shows how to use visual information for documentation, production and quality control, process monitoring, results reporting, and communication throughout the manufacturing workplace.

H. Hirano, *5S for Operators* (Productivity Press, 1996) (instructional design by Melanie Rubin).
An adaptation of Hirano's bestselling *5 Pillars of the Visual Workplace* for use in shopfloor learning and application sessions.

Teaches the basics of industrial housekeeping, the foundation for other improvement activities.

Japan Human Relations Association, ed., *The Improvement Engine: Creativity and Innovation Through Employee Involvement* (Productivity Press, 1995).
Gives a simple approach any company can use to improve processes and solve workplace problems by developing the creative resources of employees.

K. Shirose, *TPM for Supervisors* (Productivity Press, 1992) (originally published as *TPM for Operators*).
Presents the basic methodology of TPM, with a focus on operator activities to maximize equipment effectiveness.

K. Shirose, *TPM for Workshop Leaders* (Productivity Press, 1992).
Describes the hands-on leadership issues of TPM implemention for shopfloor TPM group leaders, with case studies and practical examples to help support autonomous maintenance activities.

K. Shirose, ed., *TPM Team Guide* (Productivity Press, 1995).
A Shopfloor Series book that teaches how to lead TPM team activities in the workplace and develop presentations to share improvement results.

K. Shirose, et al., *P-M Analysis: An Advanced Step in TPM Implementation* (Productivity Press, 1995).
Describes an effective step-by-step method for dealing with recurring equipment breakdowns or quality problems that happen due to multiple or combined causes.

About the Editor

The Japan Institute of Plant Maintenance is a nonprofit research, consulting, and educational organization that helps companies increase organizational efficiency and profitability through improved maintenance of manufacturing equipment, processes, and facilities. The JIPM is the sponsoring organization for the PM Prize, awarded annually to recognize excellence in companywide maintenance systems. Based in Japan, JIPM is the innovator of methodologies that have been implemented around the world. Productivity Press is pleased to be the publisher of the English editions of many of their groundbreaking publications.

About the Shopfloor Series

Put powerful and proven improvement tools in the hands of your entire workforce!

Progressive shopfloor improvement techniques are imperative for manufacturers who want to stay competitive and to achieve world class excellence. And it's the comprehensive education of all shopfloor workers that ensures full participation and success when implementing new programs. The Shopfloor Series books make practical information accessible to everyone by presenting major concepts and tools in simple, clear language and at a reading level that has been adjusted for operators by skilled instructional designers. One main idea is presented every two to four pages so that the book can be picked up and put down easily. Each chapter begins with an overview and ends with a summary section. Helpful illustrations are used throughout.

Books currently in the Shopfloor Series include:

5S FOR OPERATORS
5 Pillars of the Visual Workplace
The Productivity Press Development Team
ISBN 1-56327-123-0 / incl. application questions / 133 pages
Item # 5SOP-B267 / $25.00

QUICK CHANGEOVER FOR OPERATORS
The SMED System
The Productivity Press Development Team
ISBN 1-56327-125-7 / incl. application questions / 93 pages
Item # QCOOP-B267 / $25.00

MISTAKE-PROOFING FOR OPERATORS
The Productivity Press Development Team
ISBN 1-56327-127-3 / 93 pages
Item # ZQCOP-B267 / $25.00

TPM FOR SUPERVISORS
The Productivity Press Development Team
ISBN 1-56327-161-3 / 96 pages
Item # TPMSUP-B267 / $25.00

TPM TEAM GUIDE
Kunio Shirose
ISBN 1-56327-079-X / 175 pages
Item # TGUIDE-B267 / $25.00

TPM FOR EVERY OPERATOR
Japan Institute of Plant Maintenance
ISBN 1-56327-080-3 / 136 pages
Item # TPMEO-B267 / $25.00

TO ORDER: Phone toll-free **1-800-394-6868** (outside the U.S., **503-235-0600**), fax toll-free **1-800-394-6286** (outside the U.S. 503-235-0909), e-mail **service@ppress.com**, or mail to Productivity Press, Dept. BK, P.O. Box 13390, Portland, OR 97213-0390. Send check or charge to your credit card (American Express, Visa, MasterCard accepted). For U.S. orders add $5 shipping for first book, $2 each additional for UPS surface delivery; international customers must call for a quote. We offer attractive quantity discounts for bulk purchases of individual titles; call for more information.

See the Productivity Press online catalog at http://www.ppress.com

BOOKS FROM PRODUCTIVITY PRESS

Productivity Press publishes books that empower individuals and companies to achieve excellence in quality, productivity, and the creative involvement of all employees. Through steadfast efforts to support the vision and strategy of continuous improvement, Productivity Press delivers today's leading-edge tools and techniques gathered directly from industry leaders around the world. Call toll-free 1-800-394-6868 for our free catalog.

TPM for Workshop Leaders
Kunio Shirose

A top TPM consultant in Japan, Kunio Shirose describes the problems that TPM group leaders are likely to experience and the improvements in quality and vast cost savings you should expect to achieve. In this non-technical overview of TPM, he incorporates cartoons and graphics to convey the hands-on leadership issues of TPM implementation. Case studies and realistic examples reinforce Shirose's ideas on training and managing equipment operators in the care of their equipment.
ISBN 0-915299-92-5 / 164 pages / $40.00 / Order TPMWSL-B267

Implementing TPM
The North American Experience
Charles J. Robinson and Andrew P. Ginder

This book offers a modified approach to TPM planning and deployment that builds on the 12-step process advocated by the Japan Institute of Plant Maintenance. More than just an implementation guide, it's actually a testimonial of proven TPM success in North American companies through the adoption of "best in class" manufacturing practices. Of special interest are chapters on implementing TPM in union environments, integrating benchmarking practices to support TPM, and a requirements checklist for computerized maintenance management systems.
ISBN 1-56327-087-0 / 224 pages / $45.00 / Order IMPTPM-B267

TPM for America
What It Is and Why You Need It
Herbert R. Steinbacher and Norma L. Steinbacher

As much as 15 to 40 percent of manufacturing costs are attributable to maintenance. With a fully implemented TPM program, your company can eradicate all but a fraction of these costs. Co-written by an American TPM practitioner and an experienced educator, this book gives a convincing account of why American companies must adopt TPM if we are to successfully compete in world markets. Includes examples from leading American companies showing how TPM has changed them.
ISBN 1-56327-044-7 / 169 pages / $25.00 / Order TPMAM-B267

JIT Factory Revolution
A Pictorial Guide to Factory Design of the Future
Hiroyuki Hirano

The first encyclopedic picture-book of Just-In-Time, using photos and diagrams to show exactly how JIT looks and functions in production and assembly plants. Unprecedented behind-the-scenes look at multiprocess handling, cell technology, quick changeovers, kanban, andon, and other visual control systems. See why a picture is worth a thousand words.
ISBN 0-915299-44-5 / 218 pages / $50.00 / Order JITFAC-B267

The Visual Factory
Building Participation Through Shared Information
Michel Greif

If you're aware of the tremendous improvements achieved in productivity and quality as a result of employee involvement, then you'll appreciate the great value of creating a visual factory. This book shows how visual management can make the factory a place where workers and supervisors freely communicate and take improvement action. It details how to develop meeting and communication areas, communicate work standards and instructions, use visual production controls such as kanban, and make goals and progress visible. Includes more than 200 diagrams and photos.
ISBN 0-915299-67-4 / 305 pages / $55.00 / Order VFAC-B267

20 Keys to Workplace Improvement (Revised Edition)
Iwao Kobayashi

The 20 Keys system does more than just bring together twenty of the world's top manufacturing improvement approaches—it integrates these individual methods into a closely interrelated system for revolutionizing every aspect of your manufacturing organization. This revised edition of Kobayashi's best-seller amplifies the synergistic power of raising the levels of all these critical areas simultaneously. The new edition presents upgraded criteria for the five-level scoring system in most of the 20 Keys, supporting your progress toward becoming not only best in your industry but best in the world. New material and an updated layout throughout assist managers in implementing this comprehensive approach. In addition, valuable case studies describe how Morioka Seiko (Japan) advanced in Key 18 (use of microprocessors) and how Windfall Products (Pennsylvania) adapted the 20 Keys to its situation with good results.
ISBN 1-56327-109-5/ 312 pages / $50.00 / Order 20KREV-B267

TO ORDER: Write, phone, or fax Productivity Press, Dept. BK, P.O. Box 13390, Portland, OR 97213-0390, phone 1-800-394-6868, fax 1-800-394-6286. Send check or charge to your credit card (American Express, Visa, MasterCard accepted).

U.S. ORDERS: Add $5 shipping for first book, $2 each additional for UPS surface delivery. Add $5 for each AV program containing 1 or 2 tapes; add $12 for each AV program containing 3 or more tapes. We offer attractive quantity discounts for bulk purchases of individual titles; call for more information.

ORDER BY E-MAIL: Order 24 hours a day from anywhere in the world. Use either address:

To order: service@ppress.com
To view the online catalog and/or order: http://www.ppress.com/

QUANTITY DISCOUNTS: For information on quantity discounts, please contact our sales department.

INTERNATIONAL ORDERS: Write, phone, or fax for quote and indicate shipping method desired. For international callers, telephone number is 503-235-0600 and fax number is 503-235-0909. Prepayment in U.S. dollars must accompany your order (checks must be drawn on U.S. banks). When quote is returned with payment, your order will be shipped promptly by the method requested.

NOTE: Prices are in U.S. dollars and are subject to change without notice.

CONTINUE YOUR LEARNING WITH IN-HOUSE TRAINING AND CONSULTING FROM PRODUCTIVITY, INC.

The Productivity Consulting Group (PCG) prides itself on delivering today's leading process improvement tools and methodologies that bring rapid, ongoing, measurable results. Through years of repeat business, an expanding and loyal client base continues to recommend Productivity to their colleagues.

The PCG offers a diverse menu of products and services tailored to fit your company's needs, from focused, results-driven training to broad, world class conversion projects. Whether you need on-site consultation for a day or assistance with long-term development, our experienced professional staff can enhance your pursuit of competitive advantage.

In concert with your employees, the PCG will focus on implementing the principles of Just-in-Time (Lean Production), Total Productive Maintenance, Total Quality Management, and Total Employee Involvement. Each approach offers an array of the Productivity tools that are well-known for their significant shopfloor results: Quick Changeover, Mistake-Proofing, Kanban, One-Piece Flow, Problem Solving with CEDAC, Design of Experiments, Autonomous Maintenance, Visual Controls, Quality Function Deployment, Ergonomics, Standardization, and more.

Contact the PCG to learn how we can customize our services to fit your needs.

Telephone: 1-800-966-5423 (U.S. only) or 1-203-846-3777
Fax: 1-203-846-6883